What Makes It Taste Better

What Makes It Taste Better

by

David Wayne Hampton

Maul & Froe Press 2010

ISBN   978-0-9829973-0-7

To my dear wife Jenny,
whose support and patience made this endeavor possible

Acknowledgements

-- in gratitude to the editors of publications where these poems first appeared, some in slightly different form

"Ham Hocks" and "Aunt Beulah Sounds Off" in *Pine Mountain Sand & Gravel* 7 (Fall 1999)

"Cemetery" in *The Broad River Review* 35 (Spring 2003)

"Martha White" and "Glancing Across" in *The Broad River Review* 36 (Spring 2004)

"The Road's Been Taken" in *Pine Mountain Sand & Gravel* 11 (Fall 2004)

"Yelling Into the Mouth of a Cave" in *Appalachian Journal: A Regional Studies Review* 33:3-4 (Spring/Summer 2006)

"To Doughnuts" in *Genie* 2 (Summer 2006)

"Blackberry Tequila" in *Blueline* 28 (Spring 2007)

"A Picture's Worth" in *Pine Mountain Sand & Gravel* 12 (Summer 2007)

"The Night I Met Franklin Graham" in *Appalachian Heritage* 35:4 (Fall 2007)

"Summer Camp of Love" in *Iodine Poetry Journal* 9:2 (Fall/Winter 2008/2009)

"Eating Butterflies" in *Main Channel Voices* 5:2 (Spring 2009)

"Summer Camp Remembrance," "Mountain Stream," and "A Penny Lament" in *The Bluestone Review* (Spring 2009)

"Moon Pie by Intelligent Design" and "The American Dream" in *Pine Mountain Sand & Gravel* 14 (Fall 2010)

Contents

Eating Butterflies

I eat butterflies,
she said,
and I thought
she meant metaphorically,
like she devours the superficial facades
of people who call themselves beautiful,
the type of girl who
tears down paper rainbows,
dances through downpours,
hopping from puddle to puddle
with mischievous delight.
Her mouth was parted
and open as a morning glory.

No, she said.
I like eating butterflies.
Well, I asked facetiously,
what do they taste like, chicken?
No, like butterflies,
she said simply.
But the wings,
they are the best part
because they melt so easily
like communion wafers on my tongue,
the sweet taste of sin in the morning.
I flitted up her stairs, for coffee
and a late-night helping of sweet irony.

Cemetery

After the wave of pain
rushes through your veins
and out your heavy hands
it is replaced by a feeling
more formal than
black suits and ties
or eulogies in cold blue skies
dirt as stiff as your heart's
stubborn beat that questions
each day since century's last week

Walking down
the stillness of the ground
and the air, the road skirting around
the bare-limbed hills
disregards the line of cars
or the growing field of granite stones
rows of mossy weathered scars

Time leads us by
the still hours when we remember
as frozen plastic flowers
become faded, outlived
recollect nothing of the sun's glow
but only the visiting chill
of those who won't let go

Martha White

The first time you saw me
without my dungarees
was down by the creek.
You were wildcrafting
and I was skinny-dipping,
washing bales of hay dust
from behind my ears.
In your arms you held
a basket of Yellowroot,
which you dropped
in teary-eyed laughter
at the sight of my backside.
When you told me I was
as white as two buttermilk biscuits,
I drew close my arms,
bronzed from the elbow down,
concealing what pale skin I could
that almost glowed in the clear water.

I couldn't count the times when
my grandmother said the same thing
during childhood baths.
I sat in the wash tub, embarrassed,
with a sponge and a bar of lye soap,
watching the water turn cloudy
while she always made sure
I cleaned behind my ears,
standing above me in her gingham dress.

But you hung yours
on a rhododendron limb
along with your bloomers
and, with a cannonball splash,
jumped into the swimming hole beside me,
making sure to soak my clothes
on the opposite bank.
I smiled astonishingly,
wondering
what rock
you had been sunning yourself on
for *your* back to be so tan,
so unbroken by modesty,
and remembered how Grandma
never cared much
for buttermilk biscuits.

To Doughnuts

Doughnut, thy glaze is to me
    Like the white cliffs of Dover
That sailors spy on a weary sea.
    A crispy sweet horizon covered,
    Fried fresh and warm as a lover.

On weak cups of coffee, no foam
    To sweeten the surface of lonely brews.
Thy neon sign has brought me home
    To the rich java I once knew,
And the dip of your hot, glazed dough.

Look! in yon drive-thru window light,
    Like Prometheus the cashier stands,
    Thy caloric fire boxed in his hands.
I've come full circle for earthly delights,
    And into the Promised Land.

My Caffeine Declaration

I will brew me a fresh pot of coffee,
every day a fresh pot of coffee,
no more of that primordial ooze
that's left by the last person to make a pot.
No, I want to pour me a steaming-fresh cup
straight from the hills of Colombia, and not
from the oil pan of my gray Chevy Nova.

I will drink it black, without creamer
without sugar or powdered creamer.
I will drink heartily and without bitterness,
as the vultures swarm around my fresh kill.
Let them have what's left after I've finished
filling up my thirty-two ounce Thermos.
No beans to grind, I've had my fill.

The More the Cushion

Fat girls in fast cars
voluptuous and confident
corn-fed honeys
with curves to spare
fluffy ample lovelies
back from the tanning bed
shopping with Daddy's money

The American Dream

They built a Wal-Mart.
Two months after the auction,
three generations of family farm,
I watched with idle hands
as the ground was scoured
by a hulking, hydraulic beast
from an age before time,
all arms and teeth,
tetanus rusted, hawking soot,
scraped back the trees and grass
from the skin of the earth
like a scalded hog,
down to the rock and meat,
the red dirt and raw clay.

The rains came to soothe the wound.
It carried more dirt away,
tender seeds swept into concrete culverts
bound for the river bottom.
Little pebbles and rocks held onto nothing,
soil melting away from around them
like rendered lard from cracklings.

The earth swirled in a dream.
I stood frozen in shock,
unable to stop the bleeding,
my sluggish hands tried grasping
bales of straw, dead brush and logs,
gathering it against my body,
cobwebs to clot the cut.
Then I looked down only to find
that my body *was* the earth,
the old cow pasture, corn fields,
helplessly watched as my own fingers
gouged like bucket teeth, my flesh
scoured away with each breath,
fluid arms and elbows bent around,
excavator ghosts lunging in hunger,
pushing ribbons of pink sod and grass
from my mottled chest and back before
they poured concrete and laid cinder blocks,
when all I could do was bend over and take it.
They shoved a Wal-Mart up my ass.

Yelling Into the Mouth of a Cave

Hello
Sound
waiting to arrive
back around
down into the cracks
where the limestone
yawns great gulps
of ancient air underground
previously accustomed
to drops whispering
from mineral tongues
touching kissing
for a thousand years
in darkness crystalline
Sound
Echo

Moon Pie by Intelligent Design

When eating a Moon Pie,
should we question how it's made,
the soft marshmallow sandwich,
chocolate with graham cracker cookie?
Does it matter how it came to be?
Who tilled the soil to plant the seeds,
for the wheat, the sugar cane, the cocoa beans?
Should it matter to us how many days it rained
or how much sunshine greened the stalks and leaves,
how the grain was threshed, the cane pressed,
the cocoa beans roasted and processed,
or that it contains shortening or artificial coloring?

Why do people argue over the creation of the earth?
Though more important than a marshmallow sandwich,
does it diminish God's power if he didn't finish by Saturday?
Would it make us feel better if we were all an accidental anomaly?
Maybe the important question is a matter of perspective,
not so much how the marshmallow got here first,
but why it was created is what makes it taste better.
Does it matter that Genesis neglects to mention the details
of plate tectonics, dinosaurs, the formation of water vapor to clouds,
the sculpting of amino acids into human beings?
Like da Vinci's Mona Lisa, his own smile a model of reference,
a master craftsman shouldn't reveal the exact process
and painstaking care that went into his work.
It's mystery is priceless.

Why create unless it's to be experienced and enjoyed?
Why were we created except to create, experience, enjoy,
and to joyfully sing praises for that creation?
I imagine somewhere off a Tennessee highway
someone is hungry and staring at a Moon Pie
on a gas station shelf, next to the honey buns,
and thinking it's probably full of saturated fat,
taking their spring water and walking away,
without even checking the label, and that's okay.
But you can't deny the purpose of a Moon Pie.
It's there to delight our nose and taste buds,
chocolate, vanilla, double-decker banana,
to curb any working man's appetite.
And if you still don't believe, unwrap the plastic,
take a whiff of its sweetness, and you'll see.
Sink your teeth into a large bite,
and don't forget the RC.

A Vexing Conundrum

so much depends
on what?

and who left the
wheel barrow

out in the rain
rusting

red while they sat
inside

dreaming of chicken
dinners?

Swimming with Clothes

When I heard splashes from the beach front,
voices echoing in the summer dark,
I emptied my pockets, kicked off my shoes,
and waded in for a midnight swim.

The last night of our summer season,
after all the campers left for home,
the college staff massed in celebration,
synchronized in true Methodist fashion.

The lake water spread from me in ripples,
as I swam toward the nearest hushed voices.
"Is that you, Country?" they asked. "If so,
why are you still wearing your clothes?"

"Well, of course I'm still wearing...,"
and before I could answer I realized the error
of my impulsive action, as people cheered
for the director's son off the high-dive pier.

Like a gangly, featherless crane he flew,
every doughy limb flung to the star-lit sky,
while the nurse's aide climbed the ladder
her ample natures greeted the air with attention.

14

Had I but a warning, some anticipation,
I wonder if I would I have met the expectation
and swam out boldly, without hesitancy or clothing
among the dozen or more naked bodies?

But the shock of the lake water, perhaps
 it being the only veil that brushed between
me and everyone else's free-floating privates,
was more than my 15-year imagination could take.

I dog paddled back to shore in awkward haste
with shrunken tail between my legs, and my shirt
clung cold against the hot embarrassment in my gut.
From the darkness, the counselors' laughter echoed.

Before It Was Called the Mullet

Business up front, but party in the back
a lion's mane under a ball cap
wavy and billowing over neck and shoulders
the alpha male proclaiming his dominant nature
when stylish men didn't need to wear ponytails

Not much different than Davy Crockett's cap
rustically handsome with his raccoon tail in back
before George Clooney made popular the Julius Caesar
Billy Ray Cyrus showed us the longer the better
women had something to run their fingers through

These days the hairstyle is getting a bad rep
masculine display turned morosely unkempt
no worse than hair gel and highlights, in my opinion
as long as there's a place for professional wrestling
the Carolina Waterfall will make a comeback

Glancing Across

It must be a good book.
Her eyebrows lift and a smirk
crosses her face from time to time.
She lightly scratches the back of her neck
as if deep in thought, lost in the pages,
she adjusts the corner of her glasses.

I sip my coffee over yesterday's newspaper,
but from where I sit I can't quite see
the title of what she's reading.
Is it a mystery, a suspense,
could I be her protagonist?
Smuggle secret files to our rendezvous,
defying danger, steal a kiss.

She's looking up,
how long I can't tell.
I dart my eyes quickly
to my cup and wonder
if she noticed me.
With a slight smile
I blow casually into
my cold coffee and take a sip.

The Summer Camp of Love

I was so high that summer.
     The world was unclouded and bright.
          Taking hits off the Holy Spirit
          at the Chapel Woods campfires,
               getting ready for the bridegroom.
               Trimming our wicks, we knew.
          He was coming with sound of trumpets,
          and we would forever stand atoned.
     For those who repented of their sins,
cast their earthly vices aside,
were the first to get stoned.

The Road's Been Taken

Mountain biking alone in the woods,
Soaking in the green undergrowth,
My travels came to a stop. I stood
At a fork in the trail, which wasn't good.
This divulgence my map didn't show.

I took the one that was almost not there,
A long-abandoned, single-track trail,
To keep Nature to myself, not to be shared
With the hard-core cyclists who didn't care
If they ran over me with their Cannondales.

That morning was a calm blue day,
So peaceful and pristine I didn't look back.
Though limbs hung low and in the way,
I pedaled like a champ, I'll have to say,
When my tires came across fresh gravel pack.

A break in the trees ahead caught my eye.
What I saw from that ridge top made me wince,
A scene that would make The Lorax cry,
Red clay washouts, not a trunk stood for miles.
Diesel exhaust rose from dozers in the distance.

I stopped to gaze with utter dismay,
My quaint path vanished into logging ruts,
Tree stumps and brush piles every which way.
The sun glared through a yellow haze
Like a Martian landscape in clear-cut.

This story I guiltily recall,
Some day sitting in my new home
In a North-Charlotte suburban sprawl.
Into the woods I returned to my crawl,
And buried my indifference in the earthy loam.

Aunt Beulah Sounds Off

A pioneer-island in a world that has no use for pioneers —
the unsplit rock of Fundamentalism, calomel clan-virtues,
clannish vices, fiddle tunes and a hard God.
          --Stephen Vincent Benét

Don't call us backward.
We walk in the same direction as you,
just not in such a hurry to discard
the old for the new.
We're content with our pace, thank you.

Sure, while you may have been the first
on your block to listen to your records in stereo,
to install an 8-track player in your Pinto,
to fill your CD tower with the latest music,
we were already making our own,
hewing out tunes on fiddle, dulcimer, and banjo,
not from woofers or tweeters, but from our own hands it
          flowed.

Restless and discontent city-folk
with your throw-away culture,
media-stoked and commercially corrupt,
defiling your identity,
defining yourselves with store-bought trinkets,
and what you can't buy right away, you rent,
no money down and take years and years to pay.
I'm sorry, but that's just not our way.

And we aren't so out of touch
that we don't know
about microwave ovens and bread machines,
but biscuits rise better
in four hundred degrees
of cast iron and oak kindling.
Microwaves are good for warming coffee,
but not cold kitchens in winter.
As for chopping firewood, my callused hands can deal
    with the splinters.

Tradition is our identity,
and change does come slow, I'll admit.
But when it does, we don't forget
how we were raised, preserving,
passing on the memories
of the way things used to be.
You say it's not your bag, and that's just fine with me.

Todd, NC

Elkland, once a boom town of Watauga County,
where the railroad from Abingdon ended
to drop off passengers and load timber.
The giant engines spun on a turntable
to head back the other way.

Hotels, stores, banks, and taxi service
sprung up like mushrooms in a narrow valley,
shared by the South Fork of the New River.
Loggers and sawmills made their truck ready
to be hauled back the other way.

With the forests stripped of their hardwoods,
the Virginia-Carolina came less frequently
with nothing to haul and no one to bring.
Like locusts they swarmed to other prospects
to make their living in other ways.

The railroad gone, the tracks were taken up,
its steel sold cheaply to the Japanese,
just like New York's Sixth Avenue El,
scrap metal turned to weapons of warfare
used against our own Pacific Fleet
to send our boys to a watery grave.

Blackberry Tequila

thorn
 briars rip
  small scratches
   scored into the back
   of my sweaty hand
    just enough to bring bloody
    strands of red beaded jewels
    shine, but not near as succulent
    as the darker liquid charms
    that hang pregnant with juice
   shaded cool by thicket leaves
   slip privately into my open palm
  staining my clumsy fingers purple
 I lick between thumb and forefinger
tasting the sweet blackberry blood
sticky, with the salty tang of my own
life juices marinate with a savory sting

Open Season for Fools

Define rube – and look for my picture.
Take it with you, that Polaroid memory,
the last time I saw you – that was me,
duped into thinking we had something exceptional.

I was a tool, you used – to tighten your spine,
then dropped me in the yard, to forgotten rust.
You left me long before you didn't say goodbye.
It's the new catch-and-release program for suckers.

I am all heel, spent – my energies walking
upright like a good cad should – sinned
secretly in naive innocence at what you've done,
let you get under my thin, gullible skin.

The Night I Met Franklin Graham

Just about dusk, as the autumn sky slid
like tomato sauce over the Blue Ridge,
I delivered two pizzas to Samaritan's Purse
by mistake, intended for carryout instead.

After running to every warehouse and building,
the warming sleeves sweating from the brisk-damp air,
I found the doors locked, and decided a tongue lashing
was in order for the new guy who took the order
and sent me to the outskirts on a wasted delivery.

As I walked back in defeat, the triangle sign
illuminating the cold valley fog with its light,
a Land Rover roared hastily into the parking lot,
a holy suburban roller with tinted windows
descending, an elbow hanging out the driver's side.

Pizzas in hand, my mouth agape from excitement,
I humbly said, "Mr. Graham, it is a pleasure."
Inspired, I tried to tell him how I admired
and prayed for his missions, read his book,
wrapped Christmas shoe boxes in sealing tape
with my church youth group in junior high.

I also wanted to tell him how I, too, knew
what it was like to live in my father's shadow.
A college dropout trying to make a living,
my father a hot-shot professor at Appalachian.

"That'll be $13.50," remembering the pizzas,
I handed him his boxes through the window.
He handed me a check for the exact amount,
and with no more than a curt "Thank you,"
he ascended back into the indignant darkness
just as quickly as he first appeared.

Christ asked his disciples at the last supper
who was greater, the ones who sat at the table
or the ones who served those reclining guests.
Driving back into Boone, the fog illuminated
by the orange glow of Blowing Rock Road,
I wondered how many times might Jesus
have gotten stiffed on his delivery tips if
he had slung pies instead of breaking bread,
and took a swig of Cheerwine in remembrance.

Ham Hocks

While eating a funnel cake I saw him,
walking down from the uphill side of Main
where factory houses are stacked like cards.
That day he must have felt a little out of place
with the starched collars and tourist faces
of the Harland County Apple Festival,
tall, gray hair in a cowlick, wearing work boots
and overalls without a shirt,
looking like he had just awakened
from a third-shift-induced slumber.

I sat on a curb as he crossed the street
to a hippie vendor counting change.
"Where are your ham hocks?" he asked,
clearing sawdust from his throat with a loud hawk,
looking red-eyed and clearly confused.

"We sell *hammocks*, man – woven by Mayan Indians,"
the vendor replied with a faint smile and a nervous tug
on the shirttail of his sweater.

He spat on the ground beside him.
"I read your sign from my front porch,
walked all the way down the hill...,
aimin' to get me some ham hocks."
Hands in his pockets, the long-haired vendor
only shrugged his shoulders and smiled again.

The old man walked out into the street
among the crowds of balloons and baby strollers,
squinted his eyes at the vendor's sign above,
and scratched the stubble on the end of his chin.
He walked up to the booth once more,
stooping to get under the canvas awning.
"So you don't sell ham hocks then?"
he asked again in a querulous voice.

"Nope," the vendor answered with finality
and, almost mockingly, asked
"What are ham hocks?"

With a look like a slap in the face,
the old man backed away, bumping clumsily
into a young couple eating candy apples.
I turned to sneeze,
blowing powdered sugar off my paper plate,
but lifted my head in time to observe
the old man slip behind the vendor's booth
unnoticed by others,
hook the toe of his brogan
around a corner pole.
The falling canvas captured
the hippie and two customers
as a cowlick head of hair
sauntered away, disappearing
behind a bee-swarmed dumpster.

A Picture's Worth

Before becoming a lineman
over forty years ago
for Appalachian Power,
he went house-to-house
reading meters, which he hated.
The coveted job was in climbing poles.
Way out in the country drudgery
on a bend along the New River,
my grandfather came across
a house that once had electricity,
an old homestead abandoned.
The door was left ajar, so he called
into the dark front room
for an answer, any reply.
As he stepped in with hesitancy,
all he found was emptiness
and cigar boxes of old photos,
heaped over and spilling,
spread out in the floor,
nameless faces staring back at him
from the forsaken dust,
weathered and tired, but still smiling
with white eyes and scarecrow poses.
He dropped his clipboard,
grew sickened at the sight of
these intimate, orphaned memories,
the scattered pictures of forgotten people.

Grandpa swore he never wanted
to be like the ones in those photos,
his family left behind for some stranger
to find scattered to the elements,
curiously shuffled and nosed through,
intimacy forced through mildewed teeth.
He would rather his pictures be burned,
and their secret ashes scattered,
than left out to slowly shrivel
like so many bleached bones in the sun.

Ninety years of captured moments
sag open on the kitchen table
in shoeboxes stacked haphazardly.
My grandfather and I pore over photos.
Through my bewildered hands
pass faces I don't find familiar,
have never seen in their youth
when the world seemed black and white.
Some photos frustrate him greatly
because he can't quite trace
the tenuous connection
between memories and moments,
and there is no one else who can.
Sifting through the scalloped edges,
waiting for an answer, any reply,
we hold an informal séance
in the yellow lamplight,
for his memories to spark
a blue flame of interest in me.

(no stanza break)

We try to resurrect diligently
those whom the world has forgotten,
as time sifts them to unmarked graves.

Granny's Manicures

There was a point when I felt
I was too old at age twelve
for Granny to cut my fingernails
by the bright lamp of her recliner chair.
Her Rose Milk hands would hold each finger
while she snipped with tiny scissors.
Blades crackled through the nail grime,
curling slivers into her lap like dirty lemon rinds.
With a silver emery board she filed the corners
of my nails so I wouldn't chew the sharp edges.

When I told her how I felt,
she looked down at her hands that held
scissors and file she pulled from the table drawer,
and sat straight up from her recliner chair.
Muted astonishment filled the lines on her face,
while disappointment bobbed in its silent wake.
Granny took my rough hands in hers and smiled,
looked into my eyes with the wonder of a child,
and dubious mirth like she was trying to find
a man behind the grape mustache and dirty nail rinds.

3:15

There is a rapturous change in the air,
that everlasting moment before the bell,
whether it's in the early afternoon sun
streaming through dusty Venetian blinds or
something angelic in the sweeping moments,
the red second hand of the classroom clock,
hanging over the door like an omen,
brushing up the last minutes,
gathering the seconds, sending
waves crashing on rocky anticipation,
the zenith of crescendos, to the exact moment
desks squeak, books thunder shut,
forget your homework,
five, four,
three, two,
one

Spit Wads

Paper crinkle gives way to
a softening, soaking up
of plaque and saliva
molars chewing soberly
taste of bleach in jaw
tongue rolling dough
into little balls
no bell can dismiss
the absolute resiliency
of drawn breath
behind pursed lips
and a cafeteria straw

Before I Wake

I think I know what makes me dream
these pulpy, silo-rich travels into mountain towns,
off the main roads from the soft piedmont suburbs,
driving ahead of the kudzu progression
of four lanes that brought the Wal-Marts.

I am behind the wheel of my uncle's Chrysler
under a sky of cold gristle, pulling into
a shopping center plaza, pot hole ruts,
white parking space lines holding that last chunk of pavement,
cracks dissolved from winter's freeze and thaw.

Faded store front awnings look gray and tired,
wood shingles bleached of its mucilage sap,
but underneath, the sidewalk teems with bodies
lank and porcine, bustling in and out of the A&P
after church, meeting for lunch at the Roses cafeteria.

I walk into the grocery store and I am home again,
hit by the smell of ripe bananas and the rubber check-out conveyor,
people talking and standing around the butcher's counter.
I walk down the aisle where the stock boy wields his price gun
to check the colored twist ties for the freshest bread.

I'm here, in the shriveled flower end of an apple I didn't pay for,
hidden crust like a belly button that needed picking.
I twist the woody stem closer to my true love's letter,
then step outside the store to peer around the corner for the hills
of hazy blue and sink my mouth into their vulvate core.

But in cold embarrassment I run back inside
to discover I'm only wearing my dress sock suspenders,
and the bag boys have run out of brown paper.
Familiar eyes look through me with tourist suspicion.
Before I wake, I take my bags of ice and leave.

Finding Inspiration

It's not the eureka moment,
but the long, slow continuing,
not in the gold nugget
but in the hunching forward,
hands in the dirt and sand,
shoveling, sifting, swirling on
and not the flash in the pan.

It's the sun over our shoulder,
the mountains lifting it over the edge,
when it arrives regardless
of our effort or merit.
Accept the warmth graciously,
and try not to take the credit.

Hard Diction

Poetry Temptress!
You tease me with an inkling,
call to me like a sweet muse,
fondling my heavy thoughts
just long enough for me
to feel that familiar rise,
grabbing pen and paper,
and as the first line swells
firmly in that Eureka moment,
to what I hope will be
an explosion of words,
you leave me.

Bitch.

Thirteen Ways of Looking at a Booger

I.

Among the 20 tissues,
the only blemishes
were the smear of boogers.

II.

I was of 3 nostrils,
like the breath,
in which there were 3 boogers.

III.

The booger whirled in the autumn wind.
It was a large part of the snot rocket.

IV.

A man and a woman
are one.
A man and a booger
are alone.

V.

Do I prefer
the beauty of Kleenex
or Puffs with lotion,
the booger whistling in the nostril
or just after?

VI.

Icicle boogers hung from my nose
because I had a cold
and it was cold outside.

VII.

O thin handkerchiefs of K-Mart,
why do you think you can catch
that thick booger, those golden nuggets?
Don't you see the spoon
stirring in the neti pot?

VIII.

I know the noble nose goblins,
and I also know
where the finger hides them.

IX.

When I was seven
my last tissue blew away.
The boogers marked their edges on my sleeve.

X.

At the sight of winter,
creeping with blue light,
I knew the boogers would
soon express themselves sharply.

XI.

He drove through Eastern Kentucky
in a coal truck.
Once, the thought took him,
in that the coal dust
in his nose would be all that's left,
a Black Mountain booger.

XII.

The nose is blowing,
the boogers will soon be flowing.

XIII.

It was darkness all night.
The stars had fallen,
they all had fallen.
A booger sat on my fingernail.
I flung it to the sky.

A Penny Lament

Lincoln doesn't tarnish like he used to,
when the soft copper, mellow brown,
raised his ruddy cheekbones
through the Great Depression,
and every thumb-rubbed wish
shown on his bearded jaw line,
the Great Emancipator,
when wheat was every man's gold standard.

Some time ago they thinned his relief,
when copper became too precious
to use through and through.
His gilded coat now sullies and mars,
doesn't hold that umber patina
or warm in the hand for penny candy,
the Tin Man, with a heart of zinc,
left in the tray of a gas station counter,
forever dreaming of an Emerald City.

Summer Camp Remembrance

-1991-

The discovery was made
behind the dining hall on the bank.
Remnants of a blackberry patch
once stood seven feet high and
stretched clear to the top of the hill.
In the heat of a July weekend
we climbed through the briars, sweating
with a #10 can, and filled it to the top,
staining our fingertips purple,
eating only the largest.
The rest went into a cobbler
I tried baking to impress
that red-headed girl whose name escapes me.
She laughed, could tell I used Bisquick,
but enjoyed it just the same, I think,
with a scoop of ice cream and my company.
Her purple fingers held her spoon lightly.

-1992-

Just off the Shoals trail,
nestled against a steep bank,
there is an old spring house
built of flat rocks from the nearby creek.
An adventurous arts and crafts queen
and I discovered its secluded location,
followed its gurgling and bubbling
like it was calling out to us.
Under the wood-rot doorway
stretched a long copper pipe that trickled
cold water onto the sandy ground.
Shaded deep within its frame
in a dark, pebble-lined pool,
were five amber bottles of Pabst,
standing half submerged,
and still cold to the touch.
We could just make out the blue ribbons
from the rusty bottle caps in the sunlight.
Our cupped hands caught the clear draft
still tapped into the hillside.
The spring water tasted cold and secret,
like the sweet, cool kiss of her lips.

-1993-

The lifeguard's rowboat,
now decommissioned to rest
upturned against a sycamore tree,
once doubled as a gondola for two lovers.
A soft-faced, curly-haired girl and I
talked for hours while I steered
with the oars around the far end of the lake.
Water lapped against the banks of the shore
sending the cattails swaying with the ripples.
Her freckles were bright in the evening glow.
Though I don't remember the conversation,
I still smell the fabric softener she used
in the green flannel shirt I gave her,
and the way the light reflected off the water
around her in gold shimmers.
It took me two years of college
and a pair of glasses to realize
it was just the glare off the water.

-1995-

The revelation was made
at old Campsite 13.
It's remnants still lie hidden
just off the trail below the dam.
Underneath a soft mat of pine needles,
the fire circle sits, waiting for another spark.
We laid down on my jacket, and her poncho,
the damp ground warming under us.
Her small frame and bobbed hair
made her look like a fairy, or a wood nymph,
by the glowing flames of the campfire.
And the soft touch of her skin,
the ballet of her hands,
told me that I was her satyr.
The night was swirling, singing
with tree frogs and katydids,
dancing with the flickering shadows
beyond the growing firelight.
When I awoke in September
I found only cold, gray ashes
in the pit of my stomach.

-1996-

Down Fern Valley is the meditation trail.
A bench rests on the edge of a creek bank
where my best friend and I sat and talked.
Engaged for two years to a program assistant,
she told me she was having second thoughts,
that she had considered having an affair
with her younger co-counselor.
She spoke with surprising frailty,
this strong-willed woman, confiding in me.
I could see the confusion and worry in her eyes.
At the same time, he rode up behind us
on his mountain bike, the younger boy.
She told him to go away, for now,
that we were just fine,
just two friends talking.
I secretly wished, for more than a moment,
that she would run off with me instead,
and leave everyone else at camp behind
in a cloud of brown, gravelly dust.
I looked into her sad eyes
at the silent blue resolution,
her gaze sinking into mine.
We talked some. She sighed,
as the air in the trees gained strength.
A cool breeze up from the water
kept the mosquitoes away.
We walked back to the main lodge

(no stanza break)

eventually, and I knew
in how she held my hand,
she would be okay.

Mountain Stream

There is an orchestra of percussion
in a cold mountain stream,
the ploink, plunk, brunk,
of the water
rolling low over rocks into its deep underneath,
with acoustic off-beat to the smooth applause
of thousands of little pebbled hands,
the giddy, gurgle-gargle,
of liquids
like water nymphs chirckling from hollow logs,
the high hat, pat-a-slap tat,
of silver
slivered minnows shooting out from the current
land with the whispered tension of a brush.

There is mystery in the fluid performance,
the viscous thunder and the wind behind it.
I stretch an animal skin over hollow gourd
on the slaked banks with the mockingbird,
try to find my own rhythm, almost sapient
to the rock and roll of this sagacious world,
plug into the crickling current and play it back.
Leaf fairies whirl and shake their hips.

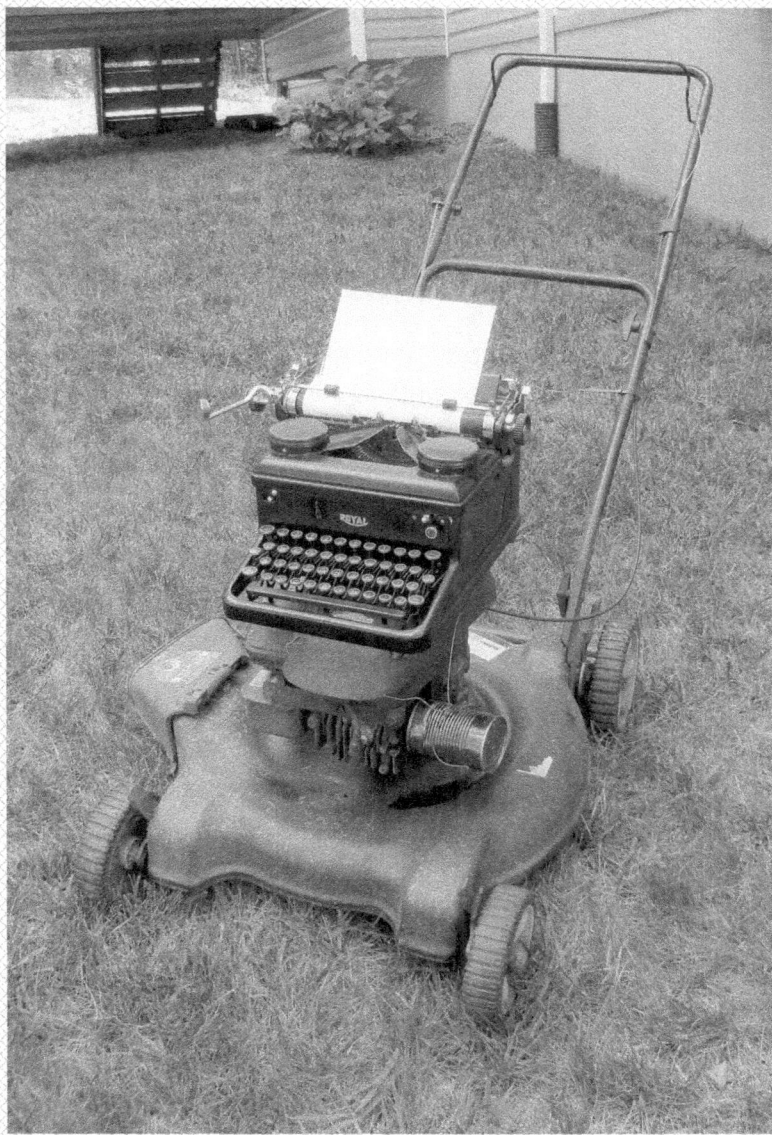

First Gasoline-Powered Typewriter, circa 1982

www.ingramcontent.com/pod-product-compliance
Lightning Source LLC
Chambersburg PA
CBHW022341040426
42449CB00006B/662